Boy from the
Black Country

Boy from the the Black Country

Andrew Read

To order additional copies of this book, contact:
Xlibris Corporation
0-800-644-6988
www.xlibrispublishing.co.uk
orders@xlibrispublishing.co.uk
300192

Contents

Introduction

My interest in poetry, especially the ones that make people smile, goes back to my formative years. As a nipper I would marvel at my Granddads poems, limericks and rhymes, some of which he himself composed.

I have been writing poems since my late teens and am constantly asked why I haven't published my work before. There is no quick answer to that question, suffice to say I am now in a position to release my debut selection.

I am dedicating this book to my lovely wife, Kay, who is supportive of everything I do, or attempt. I know how lucky I am to have Kay as my rock.

Also for my gorgeous daughter Rebecca, who prefers the moniker Becksta! Becky helped me choose most of the poems for this book, so I know I have at least one fan!

There are many more dedications dotted about the book, but for now, I hope you enjoy reading these poems as much as I enjoyed composing them.

Foreword

My recent interest in poetry is born from writing little ditties to celebrate work colleagues birthdays, marriages and the like. My compositions have been enjoyed and laughed about, just as they were intended to. I have included a couple written for such occasions, although I have generalised the poems by removing the original recipients names.

I have always enjoyed reading and listening to Pam Ayres. An Uncle of mine needs little encouragement to recite Marriott Edgars "Albert and the Lion" at family events. So impressed by the writing of Mr Edgar, I sought out other works of his and was delighted to read many more of the Ramsbothams escapades.

Why publish a book at the age of 43?
Why a book of poems?
Why not, is the answer to both questions.

I'll admit, I am not famous, nor a celebrity and outside my family, friend and work circles, I am an unknown quantity. I am just a normal (?) working class guy born and bred in Walsall, now living in Oldbury.

My upbringing, although very enjoyable, was nothing out of the ordinary. Mother, father, me and my little sister, living in a 3 bed semi-detached house on the Delves in Walsall. Dad worked, mom stayed at home (well at least until we left school). Our family was not a wealthy one, but we never went without. We were brought up to know right from wrong.

As a proper grown up family man and father of above average intelligence (so I'm told), I've always worked and I've had various 9-5 admin jobs, most of which I've enjoyed.

My life has been less than spectacular and if I'm really honest not that interesting at all really.

So, why should you be interested in anything I've written?

Friends and family have been telling me for years that I have a talent for writing poems and that I should "do something with them". I also enjoy writing songs. Mostly I enjoy making people laugh, which hopefully some of the poems in this, my first outing, will do.

I hope you will enjoy my work as I am pretty sure we have shared similar experiences and observed the same things.

We all know those people, relatives and friends, who have similar stories to tell, and if only one of my pieces of work awakes a happy memory for you, it makes this project worthwhile.

Chapter 1

Family

This first chapter is a celebration of family. All families are similar, in essence. I am sure you have experienced some of what is mentioned in this chapter.

This section is dedicated to the very people who inspired me to write.

June Read, my late mother, I miss you more with every passing day, and I know we will be together again one day. You have left me with so many brilliant memories and I know you would be more than happy for me to share them with others. I am just so pleased you were able to read some of these before your passing, and even more pleased that you enjoyed them.

Frank, Irene, Dolly and Sid, my brilliant Grandparents', who left me with so many fantastic memories. You may all be gone, but you are certainly not forgotten.

Barry Read, the best dad in the world, thanks for everything you have ever inspired me to do and all I am yet to attempt. Thanks also for the great material you've given me. I hope my work helps keep the memories alive.

Mandy Read, my favourite Li'l Sis, hope this evokes happy memories for you too. Love you.

Where's Granddad From?

It was a hot and sunny day,
The kind where sweat profused,
My Granddad gave me such a shock,
And left me so confused,
While walking to the library,
To return some books,
Four old men sat outside a pub,
Went quiet and gave us looks,
"Ah bist yer Frank" one man called,
"Oy aye tu bad" he said,
"Un ahs yer nippa" another asked,
I shook my baffled head,
"This un eers ar Andyroo,"
"Ees stoppin ferriz tay"
Then more jibberish was spoken,
And I looked the other way,
The language spoke was alien,
And it made me sullen,
Cuz in that time my Granddad changed,
From him to something foreign,
We said goodbye, at least I think,
And went about our business,
When we returned to his house,
Nan saw I was distressed,
I told my Nan what had occurred,
And asked, "Where's Granddad from?"
She explained about the Black Country,
And that he was born in Darlaston.

2am Cleaning

When my Nan and Granddad had their flat at Saddlers Court,
Once I stayed overnight and a lesson I was taught,
I chose to sleep in the lounge instead of the spare room,
A better choice would have been the closet with the mop and broom.

Granddad bade me a good night and off to bed he went,
It was nearing midnight and my energy was spent,
As I bedded down to sleep because it was so late,
Nan put on the TV to watch Prisoner Cell Block H.

She peeled herself an apple and offered me its skin,
I sluggishly refused due to the state that I was in,
I remember drifting in and out of a half slumber,
Then Nan offered me a sandwich of cheese and cucumber.

I do not recall answering but a sandwich did appear,
I left it so my Nan did proceed my platter to clear,
As I returned to the warmth of the oncoming sleep,
I heard the TV switch off with its inimitable peep.

Then I heard noises of a spray can being discharged,
The odour of Mr Sheen the atmosphere did charge,
Nan was polishing at 2am to beat her boredom,
Scratching at stubborn bits with her fingers and her thumb.

I tried to keep my eyes closed to con my body into sleep,
As Nan continued on with her trusty dusters to sweep,
Finally the cleaning stopped and silence did ensue,
I was drifting back off when suddenly out of the blue.

A tapping on my left shoulder through the quilt I felt,
Tears of tiredness welled up as my eyes began to melt,
I heard my Nan repeat my name like she was in distress,
And as I stirred she said, "Are you asleep? Good night, God bless"

Nan, as all Nans' do, spoiled me rotten, which explains why I'm a chocoholic today!

Nan's Golden Tin

Every Sunday morning, I was dropped off at my Nan's,
To have a dinner with her, Granddad, my Sister and Cousins,
I never missed a Sunday, it was my weekly treat,
And I was always very good all my dinner I would eat,
This was followed by pudding and squash or lemonade,
My favourite was the sweet pink and yellow Battenburg cake,
But for me this was the intro, the prelude if you please,
To the main event which never failed to appease,
Into the kitchen Nan would go to retrieve that golden tin,
Which held far greater treasures than those sought by Aladdin,
For kept inside were chocolate bars and other things so sweet,
And we could take whatever we wished as long as we could eat,
The inside of the golden tin was always clean and bright,
All the wrappers looked like jewels glowing in their light,
Many happy times were spent dipping in that golden tin,
I'm so proud my daughter had the chance to dive right in.

I am ashamed to confirm that this actually happened and even more so that there was no need to exaggerate this story. I still have nightmares. I still have the stretch-marks too.

Having Nan's that were good close friends was normally advantageous. This was one time it was less so.

Never Again

Mother, when I was younger, was a sales agent,
For Littlewoods catalogue for which she got 1 percent,
One day a parcel was received that was ordered for her mother,
She asked me to deliver it because there was no other,
So on my Grifter I climbed and furiously rode,
With the parcel for my Nan a very cumbersome load,
Within 15 minutes I had reached my destination,
I took the short cut cycling by the Bescot Railway Station,
As I arrived Nan was cooking Roe, Fairies and Peas,
She asked me if I wanted some my answer was "Yes please"
Shortly this favourite of mine landed on my lap,
Accompanied by lots of buttered Nimble bread and baps,
An hour or so after this and a pint of tea,
I was thinking it was very nearly time to leave,
Still feeling very full and tired it was only half past one,
I left to visit my other Grandparents who lived next door but one,
Granddad opened the front door and out the aroma flew,
Nan was cooking a family favourite dumplings and stew,
It was here that I made my terrible mistake,

When offered stew for dinner I said I'd already ate,
Granddad sat there in his chair and smiled for he knew well,
That if I'd eaten at my Nan's I must eat here as well,
The largest bowl of stew quickly appeared before me,
With six of the stodgiest dumplings that you'd ever wish to see,
I did not want to upset Nan so I forced down this meal,
My stomach had stretched so much it no longer looked real,
I was so uncomfortable and felt a lot of pain,
I knew I would not be able to cycle home again,
Nan phoned Dad and explained and they all thought it a hoot,
He then came to fetch me and my bike went in the boot,
He laughed as he could not believe how I'd been such a prat,
I vowed that never again would I make a mistake like that.

We were a family of cat lovers. Over the years we had three cats, Bowsy, Tizzy and Sophie. Bowsy was by far the best cat anyone could wish for. In fact she was purrfect (sorry!). Bowsy is the cat in this poem.

Where's the Cat?

"Where's the cat?" My mother asked, while trying to call her in,
Coaxing with the munchies box, she did make such a din,
Looking out into the night while trying to spy her eyes,
Straining hard to hear out for any muffled cries,
We were in the living room, my dad, sister and me,
Dad was dropping off to sleep while sat on the settee,
With legs crossed out in front of him, adorned in denim flares,
Mom asked for assistance, sounding a bit scared,
"Can you go and check the shed?" mom asked with a sigh,
Dad mumbled his tired response, as he rolled his eyes,
Up he stood, the cat fell down, the left leg of his jeans,
She looked up so indignantly, like he'd disturbed a dream.

I was afraid of spiders when young. In fact I was scared of any type of creepy crawly thanks to Mom. If I'm totally honest, spiders still freak me out today. Read the following and you'll know why.

Arachnophobia

Whilst I am sitting here, minding my own business,
A big fat hairy spider comes and I start to feel distressed,
I know this fear's irrational, that I'm hundreds of times bigger,
And I've genuinely tried to work it out but still have failed to figure.
I think it stems back to a time when I was just a nipper,
My mother was scared stiff of them and she'd squash them with a slipper,
And then there was that fateful night, when I was in my bed,
Only to be woken by a broom above my head.
A spider crawled across my face whilst I was asleep,
And mother in her wisdom thought the spider she would sweep,
I was woken by the touch of bristles on my nose,
Just in time to see the culprit dash under the bedclothes.
Somehow mother managed to get the spider on the broom,
Then do a nifty three point turn and exit from my room,
She calmly descended the stairs and kept it at arms length,
Being very careful not to drop the bugger as she went.
There were other times that dad would catch a spider in his hand,
Then have to come and show me cos he could not understand,
How a son who towered above him, could really be so frightened,
Of such a little thing, he hoped that he would be enlightened.
I know my fear's unfounded, but I cannot start to think,
Of why I freeze and tingle, when I see one in the sink,
I think it's cos they have eight legs, and there's nothing else around,
That looks as alien as them, at least not that I've found.
I'm thirty eight years old, and my phobia depresses,
That when a spider does appear, my body and mind stresses,
I cannot rest until it's dead, it becomes my only target,
I'll step on it and squash it, 'til it becomes one with the carpet.
Oh bugger where's that spider gone, the one that got me thinking,
It's gone off into hiding, it must have had an inkling,
Of what was coming if it didn't disappear from view,
Now I won't get a wink of sleep through worrying, will you?

I have a very vague recollection of seeing an old tin bath when my Grandparents lived in their terraced house on Pleck Road. Mom told me some stories about bath night in her house. I am just hoping that my ode to the tin bath is a true reflection of what happened on bath night.

The Tin Bath

Back in the days when my parents were kids,
Just after the war when it all hit the skids,
The old tin bath would be hauled down from the wall,
And mother would boil enough water for all,
Sat there in front of a great roaring fire,
The youngest were first to remove their attire
The older you were the longer you waited,
For the Sunday night bath was so anticipated,
Mother retrieved the carbolic soap,
Then proceeded to scrub, no there was no hope,
That you have time to enjoy or be lucky,
With a relaxing hot soak or a play with your ducky,
Parents went last when the kids went to bed,
In fresh clean nightclothes, on crisp pressed bedspreads,
Once finished the tub was removed from the hearth,
And the water was emptied out in the back yard,
Poor folk used this for the Monday clothes wash,
If you had a twin tub you were considered posh,
When done the tin bath went where it was before,
Up on the wall, near the outside loo door.

As a kid, I enjoyed all sports, which given our modest back garden in Blackthorn Road, is no surprise really.

Who needs the Crucible?

Who needs the Crucible when you've got a large back lawn?
A flat green surface for my snooker table to adorn,
All throughout the summer you could see where we'd been playing,
Around where the table stood, we'd walked a light brown ring.

Who needs Wimbledon Centre Court when you've got our back garden?
During long hot summers when the ground was dry and hardened,
Taking places either side of a wind breaker net,
We would play our matches over 3 and sometimes 5 sets.

Who needs Wembley Stadium when we could play out back?
For "3 and in" and "World Cup" all my mates would pack,
We'd drive my parents crazy as we'd play out there for hours,
We'd knock panels out the fence and trample on the flowers.

Who needs Lords or Trent Bridge, when on a summers day,
With cricket bat and tennis ball the French type we would play,
Now as you know it's not about hitting 6's and 4's,
But most our time was spent retrieving the ball from next door.

If there was no sight of breeze, then badminton we'd play,
The first sign of a gust of wind would blow the cock away,
Other times we would just sit or lie there on the ground,
Telling jokes and having fun and making farting sounds.

My parents kept a great garden for us to play our games,
And at the end of every day my dad would do the same,
For he'd walk up the garden to assess the damage done,
Then stroll back to the kitchen to ask me who had won.

Running in the Park

When I was just 5 years old,
My sister would be 3,
To Walsall Arboretum,
Our parents took us for our tea,
Mum made up a picnic,
And a blanket duly laid,
It was then my little sister,
A break for it she made,
Off she ran towards the Grange,
Mum had a panic attack,
"Go and get her will you love?"
Dad said "She'll soon be back"
On she ran, she wouldn't stop,
She did not care one jot,
Dad then took off after her,
When she became a dot,
Several minutes later,
Dad and sis returned,
He was absolutely done,
But a lesson here was learned,
Mum undressed my little sis,
Who was now wet through,
There was a need to calm her down,
Her legs still kicking too,
A precedent was set that day,
And sis did not repent,
For over forty years now,
She's been independent,
Whenever we are together,
We'll often have a lark,
And I will always remind her when,
She went running in the park.

My nans were the best of friends and lived only two doors apart during the last few years of their lives. They would visit our house for tea once a week and whenever I visited them, woe betide me if I didn't visit both houses.

The Gruesome Twosome

The title of this ditty is an affectionate term,
For two lovely old ladies whose friendship was always firm,
Anyone who met them saw sisters who were so close,
But they merely were in-laws and better friends than most,
Bingo was a love they shared and they went twice a week,
And share winnings between them and they probably shared a seat,
When they went to watch the band they'd soon get up to dance,
Around their handbags on the floor like they were in a trance,
They lived two doors from each other so were always making plans,
I was the very luckiest, oh how I miss my Nans.

For as long as I can remember, my Nan kept Budgerigars. As I recall, they were nearly all called Joey, and all learned to talk (not that they had much choice). This one, however, had the greatest vocabulary of all.

Wotcha Doin?

Dolly taught her budgie to speak,
He'd learn a new word every week,
Within a year her little Joey,
Had an extensive vocabulary.

Late one day the rent man came,
And Joey played a little game,
When Dolly went to get her purse,
He spoke, he whistled, then he cursed.

"Wotcha doin?" said the bird,
The man looked around a bit unnerved,
There was no one in the room but him,
He found it quite unsettling.

"Watcha doin?" the bird repeated,
The rent man started overheating,
He scanned the room in a fit of rage,
But didn't see Joey in his cage.

"Wotcha doin?" again came the voice,
The guy half turned he had no choice,
But as he did footsteps were heard,
The sublime now became absurd.

"Wotcha bloody doin?" the voice now screamed,
This was the very worse of dreams,
Dolly laughed as she entered the room,
And saw the rent man looking doomed.

"Was that you speaking?" asked the man,
"No, my budgie speaks, he can"
And as he turned, the cage he saw,
"Wotcha doin?" Joey said once more.

Can't you tell?

When my little girl was born,
My mother-in-law was there,
Because after having two herself,
She knew what to expect, that's fair.

Mom-in-law was a great help,
In keeping my wife sane,
Especially as her daughter,
Was suffering in such pain.

Now by having one of each,
You think she'd know the difference,
Between the two genders,
Without the need for conference.

When the baby finally appeared,
She said "A boy, oh Lord",
I said "Can't you tell, she is a girl,"
"That's the umbilical chord!"

I love my wife and she says she loves me, although sometimes things happen that make me wonder. See what you think about this explanation!

Late night attack

Being rudely woken up at half 3 in morn,
My eyes focused on my wife who lay there all forlorn,
Gathering my senses as I slowly start to lumber,
Having been ripped from my all encompassing slumber.

My wife proceeded to recall her very violent dream,
Where a burglar'd broken in and she'd stifled a scream,
We quietly crept down the stairs and spied on the intruder,
Rifling through our belongings, he couldn't be any ruder.

We'd decided he'd not get away so upon him we jumped,
I held him in a full nelson, while wifey went to thump,
She drew back and launched a wicked right cross to his head,
But as all this was just a dream, she pummeled me instead.

I regain my faculties from this sense of reeling,
Taking in the story and seeing how she was feeling,
The right cross received to my neck still had me in a spin,
I told her "Next time, don't hit me, bloody well hit him".

My Granddad loved nothing more than fresh seafood. Well at least until this happened.

Whelks!

While on holiday in Westward Ho!
We decided to the rock pools we would go,
Granddad needed all our help,
To pick some of his favourites, whelks.

With buckets in one hand, net in the other,
Grandparents, me, sis, father and mother,
Marched on down, a military platoon,
To bring our enemy an early doom.

Hours passed with buckets filled,
Not knowing if they would be boiled or grilled,
Most probably they would be boiled,
But they'd be nice after all we toiled.

The whelks transferred to one container,
With water to keep them fresh for later,
"We'll have them tomorrow for tea I think",
Said Granddad putting them under the sink.

Next morning we heard mom yell,
And bolted down the stairs as well,
Downstairs looked a pile of shit,
The whelks had made a break for it.

The 6 of us spent the next 2 hours,
Retrieving whelks then cleaned and scoured,
Granddad washed and cooked then ate,
Each one that made it to his plate.

Later that day we heard him chide,
As the whelks retaliated from inside,
Then with pain he was in fits,
As he suffered with the thrupenny bits

Leave the Sheep alone

One day while out walking,
Laughing and talking,
Mom, dad, sister and me,
Mom looked around,
Li'l sis made no sound,
In fact was nowhere to be seen.

We were so worried,
We scampered and hurried,
While shouting and bawling her name,
And although she annoyed,
With our senses she toyed,
Without her life wouldn't be the same.

Up and down the lane,
Oh where was this pain,
That I now lovingly call sis,
But dad kept his poise,
Because he heard a noise,
And realised nothing was amiss.

Two fields away,
There was sister at play,
We looked at each other and moaned,
Sheep running and bleating,
Dad set off feet fleeting,
Shouting "Leave the sheep alone!"

My Daughter

When my little girl was born,
I felt that I could touch the moon,
Now she has reached 14 years old,
How did we get here so soon.

It seems like only yesterday,
I was changing dirty nappies,
And soothing gums with Bonjela,
When she was very crabby.

Most memories make me laugh,
Although I am quick to admit,
I really did not enjoy,
The projectile vomit.

And the time she sucked my toe,
Thinking it was her thumb,
I laughed so hard, she pulled a face,
And fell backwards on her bum.

I'd die for my little girl,
So all you boys out there beware,
You will have to deal with me,
If you don't treat her with special care.

Dad's Green Grub

When I was a teenager,
My father changed his car,
He bought a Talbot Sunbeam,
His favourite one by far.

There was no colour quite like,
At least none I've ever seen,
Because it was like toxic snot
The pusest of all greens.

You could easily spot it,
From a distance of 10 miles,
And it's canary yellow stripe,
Never failed to raise a smile.

Affectionately named the grub,
It was certainly no thriller,
It looked about as sporty,
As a well fed caterpillar.

The horn was so embarrassing,
A little mousy squeak,
It pained me to get in the thing,
More than once a week.

With a puny engine,
The grub was not a flier,
When dad sat there revving it,
Sounded like a hairdryer.

The fiercest part of the vehicle,
Was its aggressive clutch,
Because when depressed a millimetre,
That was far too much.

And if the clutch bite wasn't right,
The windscreen you'd go through,
The pedal temperamental,
And the car would kangaroo.

But my dad adored that car,
And he admitted that he picked,
This particular type,
As it would never be nicked.

Many weekends were spent at some club or other watching the Sounds of Z, one of the best bands in the Midlands clubland. They went down well everywhere they played and were usually fully booked Friday, Saturday and Sunday nights.

Sounds of Z

Many years ago,
When I was just a little boy,
Dad was in the Sounds of Z,
A band richly employed,
By local pubs and clubs alike,
To entertain their crowds,
So they would play their rock n roll,
But never played too loud.

Cliff did lead guitar and vocals,
The front man if you please,
His fingers dancing on the neck,
As melodies he'd tease,
From ELO to Chuck Berry,
Cliff could play them all,
And all were played note perfectly,
He was always on the ball.

Bernard was the bass player,
And sang a bit as well,
Playing live he did enjoy,
As anyone could tell,
From the first song to the last,
He could not stop dancing,
When he sang the ballads,
It was as if he was romancing.

Dad backed up with rhythm guitar,
And well placed ooh's and aah's,
Sorted out their play lists,
Whether they played near or far,
He kept a constant rhythm,
And was always bang in time,
He had his job and did it well,
Verging on the sublime.

They'd no need for a drummer,
A drum machine kept the beat,
Easily turned off and on,
By a switch laid at dads feet,
A hundred different settings,
Programmed using several knobs,
Ensuring the right beat was used,
Was one of my dads jobs.

The Sounds of Z played 15 years,
And entertained all ages,
Any money earned from this,
Helped supplement their wages,
It didn't matter where they played,
If the songs were fast or slow,
They always had to have a break,
So the crowds could play bingo!

Chapter 2

The Black Country

This chapter includes a selection of poems that give an insight into the people, language and places of the Black Country, a place I am so proud of.

The people are among the friendliest anywhere in the world, and that's not me being biased. Many people I've encountered during my life have said exactly the same.

The lingo is something else altogether. It is not just the accent that confuses outsiders, but more so the speed at which we speak.

Yow may need an interpritter fower this seckshyun, but offink yowl injoy em ennyways.

There is also a look back at yester-year, with odes that are drawn from stories told me by older relatives and friends. I hope these will conjure up a trip down memory lane for you.

Famous? From the Black Country

Many great people have
Hailed from the Black Country
And I am taking time out
To regale a tale or three.

Julie Walters comes from Smethwick,
I'm sure you must have seen,
The funniest things on TV,
Are those in which she's been.

Duncan Edwards, from Dudley,
Would have been the best,
Footballer of any age,
To wear an England vest.

Bob Warman hails from my home town,
He anchors Central News,
Suave, sophisticated, cool,
He never blows a fuse.

Author Jerome K Jerome,
From Walsall was the bloke,
Who wrote the literary great,
Three Men in a Boat.

Soul diva Beverly Knight,
Wolverhampton born and raised,
Is one of our greatest singers
And won many accolades.

Funny man Lenny Henry,
Comes from Dudelye,
He will make you laugh so hard,
You'll laugh until you cry.

William Perry born in Tipton,
And none came more brasher,
As he was the champion prize fighter,
Known as the Tipton Slasher.

Tommy Mundon from Halesowen,
Is known for his razor wit,
He'll have you rolling in the aisles,
And your sides will split.

These are just a few examples,
Of people listed to date,
Who have gained their fame,
And made the Black Country great.

Walsall Illuminations

The Walsall Illuminations I can confirm are no more,
The daft sods on the council say it's outdated, you sure,
I have many memories of going to see the lights,
Many happy hours were spent in the Arbo at night.

We used to be so proud of them, in days gone by,
Second only to Blackpool, you would here the people cry,
One thing that we didn't know, we didn't have a clue,
There was only us and Blackpool, we were the bottom of two.

One year I was out with friends just dossing round the Delves,
Wrapped up warm in Parka coats resembling lost elves,
Bright green laser lights were seen shooting up toward the skies,
Was it the start of the War of the Worlds, we couldn't believe our eyes.

The Walsall lights were definitely worth every penny paid,
As you entered the Arboretum, night turned into day,
The illuminations were a community event,
Please, please bring them back as it was our money well spent.

The Way we Spake

They say the Black Country's dialects dieing,
I'd hate to see it go,
So please read out the following,
If you are ever around Darlo.

Ow's ya bin, am yo awrite,
Is a greeting to another,
Wot ya doin ya silly cow,
You don't say to your mother.

Am yo from rahndabahts ere,
You'd say to an outsider,
Am yo bovvered weer I cum,
You'd say when you're inside her.

Duz ya wanna bosted clock,
You'd say before a fight,
Fancy cummin for a sup,
Means you'll take her out tonight.

Whooers an stinkers gerron,
Means your life is not going well,
Oll rip ya bastad faerce off,
Say's you are going to raise hell.

Get sum scran dahn yer larrup,
Means have a bite to eat,
Cum an av a butchers hook,
Has nothing to do with meat.

Woss gooin on rahnd eer then,
Means what is there to do,
Weers ya bog I wanna crap,
Means you're dieing for a poo.

Om gooin aht wi mi mucka,
Means your going to meet a friend,
I bay suwer wot day omin,
Says you're going round the bend.

Om up an dahn loik an ooers draws,
Says you've experienced highs and lows,
Stop ferrittin wi ya Cannock,
Means stop picking your nose.

Duz ya babbee wan sum suck,
You are offering some sweets,
O cud ate an oss an iz jocky,
You're starving and need to eat.

As you can see it would be a shame,
If this tradition was to break,
Because I think you'll all agree,
It's a bostin way we spake.

Late Night Encounter

Very late wun Frydee noyt, I wuz walkin back thru Carma,
I crost thu street cuz I saw a gairl un day wonna alarmer,
She terned arahnd so suddenlee, un startid cumin marway,
O fort er may be Brahms un Lizst, cuz er lukked loik er did sway,
Now az er got abit nearer, er day seem loik no lukka,
So arwuz shockt un stund when er towd me she wuz a hukka,
Oy asked er ow much she charged men wen er sold er wears,
Er sed "a pahnd a goo on the flower, un ten pahnd up the stairs",
Oy offud er a tenner and er led me to the dower,
O sed "yow am misterken bab, o wan ten guz on the flower".

Walsall's top meeting place was a stone Hippo stationed outside the Lloyds Bank at the bottom of Park Street.

The Hippo

Got to dial the number right,
Have got to meet this girl tonight,
If I get through now, I think I might,
Meet her at the Hippo.

The phone line crackles into life,
I hear her voice, so sweet and light,
I'm thinking she could be my wife,
If I meet her at the Hippo.

We agree to meet at half past eight,
I'm rushing round so I'm not late,
Knowing my luck I'll have to wait,
With the others at the Hippo.

I get there at a quarter to,
Bursting cuz I need the loo,
Trust me to need a number two,
While I'm waiting at the Hippo.

Running back I feel incensed,
It stank in that convenience,
And I wasted 10 whole pence,
But I must get to the Hippo.

Sitting, waiting patiently,
It's very nearly eight thirty,
I look around but still can't see,
My date here at the Hippo.

It is then I realize,
I've seen her once with my own eyes,
I start to feel demoralized,
While waiting at the Hippo.

Watching women come and go,
Do I smile, will they know,
I am nervous she won't show,
I'll be alone here at the Hippo.

Just as I turn homeward bound,
I hear a voice and turn around,
I see her face and my heart pounds,
And I kiss her at the Hippo.

Salt of the Earth

Black Country fowk am the sult o the airth,
We am gud nayturd un so full o mairth,
We wud du ennyfin for a true frend in need,
We wud even giya the milk aht ar tae.

Weel alluz luck aht fower ar nayburs un frends,
Un weel orl stond tugetha royt up tu the yend,
Luvverly peepul hu dow geeyer stroif,
An wen yow befriend uz, yowam won fer loif.

Wether from Tippun or Dudlye or Lye,
Weel mek yow loff but we wow mek yow croy,
Mek shuer yow dow annuy uz, cuz yow will foind aht,
Wot appuns wen yow mess the Black Country abaht.

Dow corl uz Brummies, cuz that meks uz mad,
We ay that snobbish, deluwdid or sad,
We yam wot we yam, we put orl uthers ferst,
Weem Black Country fowk un the sult o the airth.

Everyone knows a family like the Bulls. A typical ASBO type family. I have to admit, although I too know families of this ilk, I have not based the Bulls on any one family in particular.

The Bulls meet Jezza

I hate watching TV,
Unless I'm watching sport,
But today I viewed Jeremy Kyle,
And this I must report,
The first couple on the show, the Bulls,
I think hailed from Blackheath,
A very handsome pair they were,
Who between them shared ten teeth,
Mr Bull was covered in tattoos,
All dingy brown,
Mrs Bull in make up,
Looked like Pennywise the clown,
He was dressed in denims,
He was dressed to kill,
She adorned a mini dress,
Which made me feel quite ill,
The purpose of their appearance,
Was for a DNA test,
Because their sixteen children,
May not be his she confessed,
It transpired that over 20 years,
She'd slept with others,
Then had the nerve to accuse him,
Of sleeping with her mother,
Vehemently denied of course,
They'd do a lie detector test,
Then for the DNA samples,
He handed his soiled pants and vest,
Jeremy looked square at me,
And said "We will be back",
"To find out the very real truth,
buried in this pile of cack",

And sure enough they did return,
From the commercial break,
So put us out their misery,
I screamed for Christ's sake,
Jeremy held the cards aloft,
Answers to this tale of woe,
I wished he'd bloody hurry up,
Cuz I'd really got to go,
He was the father of the kids,
And he knew this of course,
But for her indiscretions,
He demanded a divorce,
He'd not slept with her mother,
This too was obvious,
As the audience applauded,
Mrs Bull screamed and cussed,
Jeremy lost his temper,
And flew into a rage,
Then asked them both to leave,
And they were cheer booed off the stage,
"Rejoin us after the break,
we've lesbians with babies,
and an 88 year old Granny,
who thinks she has got rabies"
At that I turned the TV off,
For I could endure no more,
And waited for the sport to start,
And enjoy life as before.

As a kid, I loved reading Marvel and DC comics. As I've grown older, the fascination with superheroes remains the same, although I am no longer a subscriber to the comics.

If like me, you have ever wondered what locally based superheroes are would be like, then you really need to get a life and go out more.

I am hoping to develop these characters more in the future, but purely in a literary sense.

Black Country Superheroes

Law enforcement in the year of 2215,
Is carried out in the Black Country by the Central Hero Team,
Six individuals blessed with superhuman powers,
Who took up this mantle cuz it offered full time hours.

Lead by the Dudley Dumpertruck, who lifts the heaviest with ease,
Then the Stourbridge Snotter and his amazing hurricane sneeze,
The Walsall Whizz is so damn fast he gets there yesterday,
And the Bilston Brainer who with your grey matter will play,
The Cradley Crow who effortlessly soars high in the sky,
And finally the Tipton Telescope and his x-ray eye,

Working as a close knit team, the streets are kept much safer,
In Spandex, Rubber and Lycra, which we all know can chafe yer,
My role here in all of this is merely to report,
About their famous exploits and how the bad are caught,
In this now anarchic world police try to no avail,
But with help from our heroes, good will always prevail.

The mens toilets in Walsall town centre were not the most pleasant place to do your ablutions. Do not despair. I can confirm that all public loos are pretty much the same.

Public Convenience

Please explain why it is there's urine on the floor,
Skid marks on the toilet seats, graffiti on the door,
Locks that don't work properly, if they exist at all,
Cisterns that don't flush, and no toilet roll on the wall.

Why is it the stench will always permeate your clothes,
So half an hour later strangers turn away their nose,
You're smelling like a tramp who has soiled his underpants,
You were going out on the pull, go home you've got no chance.

And why is it that some people really feel the need,
To drop their fag end in the trough right after they have peed,
And why there is a cleaner sitting behind his glass façade,
Watching what is going on, is cleaning up so hard?

And why is it that sometimes I go and stand there at the ready,
And aim so very carefully I try to take it steady,
Then some blurt decides that he's worked up a head of steam,
And I look on helplessly as the trickle becomes a stream.

I can't believe what's happening although I try to muse,
Just why he felt it necessary to go and soak my shoes,
It is more than enough to make a grown man sob,
Why do I always end up standing next to thunderknob.

And then there is the other sort who attach the garden sprinkler,
So their urine squirts outwards, they're such a messy tinkler,
These guys are the prats who spray you, oh what a pain,
When you leave the loo you look like you've been out in the rain.

And why is it I sometimes see a head above the door,
Do these people not believe in standing on the floor,
Why do they have to stand and aim from way up high,
Are they practicing to bang one out up in the sky.

And why do some just pull their flies and leave the Convenience,
Leaving without washing hands should be made an offence,
Because they spread the germs they splashed when handling their willy,
And end up spreading norovirus through being so damned silly.

Insanity

Apparently as the story goes,
The girl removed her attire,
It was December the 11th,
I swear I'm not a liar.
She ran down Blackheath High Street,
Slapping at her hips,
And stormed into the Rowley Fryer,
Demanding Fish and Chips.
Into the pub she ventured,
And punched a young man there,
A huge bar brawl did soon ensue,
As she yanked out all her hair.
She ran right into Woolworths,
The clock had just struck six,
She re-arranged the magazines,
CD's and pick 'n' mix.
She ran up to the newsagents,
And burst in through the door,
She stood there by the counter,
And pissed over the floor.
She ran down to the island,
And jumped out at a bus,
The driver slammed his anchors on,
And everybody cussed.
The police proceeded to arrive,
And chased the girl around,
She was caught by Sainsbury's,
An errant trolley brought her down.
The poor girl she was sectioned,
Although she tried to plea,
They put her in a padded cell,
Just next door to me.

Yow Cor

Yow cor goo aht drest loik that,
Yowl ketch yer deth o cowd,
Yower skerts tu short, yower pants tu long,
Yower onny sixteen years owd.

Yow cor goo aht weeaht a coot,
Yowm showin orl yer belly,
Yower piercin's looking septic,
Yower nayval's gerrin smelly.

Yow cor goo aht in shooers so high,
Theez werds O wish yowd eed,
Woy not wear sumfin sensibul,
Yowl end up wiya nosebleed.

Yow cor goo aht in a top so small,
The cowd itull be felt,
Thers mower cloff on me ankercheef,
O wear a woider belt.

Yow cor goo aht in orl that slap,
Yow look just loik a clowen,
Do yower lips need ter be that red?
Is yower ferce really that browen?

Yow cor goo aht looking so owd,
Tartish, brash and flairty,
Yowd berrer goo un chernge royt now,
Or yowm grahndid til yowm thairty.

Chapter 3

Owd Fowk

This chapter focuses on the older generation, the good, the bad, the funny, the idiotic and the downright irritating. I know these poems are not indicative of all OAP's, but you have to admit, there area hell of a lot of miseries about.

Don't get me wrong, I will be old one day, but hopefully I'll grow old gracefully and with some dignity, unlike the small number of pensioners who inspired the poems in this chapter.

They do say you can't beat pensioners . . . . That's a pity.

Where's It Gone

Where's it gone, I had it here, a couple of seconds ago,
I put it down, just down there, now where'd the bugger go,
I can't believe it's disappeared, vanished into thin air,
It must have done cos it has gone, I know I put it there.

I've racked my brain trying to think of what has occurred,
I have retraced my steps, but my memory is still blurred,
I look around impatiently hoping I will spy,
What it is I'm looking for with my eagle eye.

But what it is I'm looking for, has totally escaped me,
And what I was hoping to do, has also gone you see,
For it seems that in the panic of looking for that thing,
The last ten minutes of my life my memory has been erasing.

I have no clue of what has passed the last ten minutes or more,
And I am left with no option but to stare down at he floor,
What a div I am for not being able to remember,
But there is not a spark upstairs, not even a dieing ember.

Suddenly deflated I am by this bleeding mess,
My fingers work my temples as though they're trying to press,
The memory from whichever cranny it is hid,
I can't believe what's happened, god I think I've hit the skids.

I am too young to lose what few marbles I have left,
The way I'm going, of any thought I will soon be bereft,
Dementia must be setting in I don't know what I'll do,
Before too long my mind will be nothing more than goo.

Just as the dark clouds form, something quite strange happens,
My stomach churns quite violently and everything upends,
For now I know exactly what I was about to do,
Because I fart and almost very nearly follow through.

Now I remember thinking about sitting on the pan,
And with the paper I would do the crossword if I can,
A pen was in my pocket yes I was almost set,
But I couldn't find my readers, and I still had not yet.

Now was not the time for looking if the truth be told,
Because my body's yelling there's a fire in the hold,
I rush up to the bathroom and make it just in time,
The world crashes into my toilet, the feeling is sublime.

As I sit detoxing my reflection I do spy,
And what the mirror shows me brings a tear to my eye,
I laugh and laugh and roar so loud I think I'll end up dead,
Because the readers I searched for are perched upon my head.

OAP's and Hair

When we reach a certain age, our bodies go to pot,
Our ears and nose grow larger, and fill with hair, a lot
Unfortunately the hair on our heads speedily recedes,
But lags our orifices, like that's something that we need.

When you talk to an OAP, you spy their nostril hair,
It is so thick you can no longer tell if they are flared,
Great tufts stick out of each ear though they don't look the same,
You can't take your eyes off them, like a moth drawn to a flame.

Lovely little old dears with hair sprouting out of moles,
Clamouring for veet or immac, fighting in their droves,
To get the ointment needed to remove these follicles,
Failing that its tweezers for these tufts of fur to pull.

More hair pokes through stockings because they cannot shave,
You offer them a strimmer but are told to behave,
Obviously old folk are constantly under attack,
Becoming more and more hirsute like an ageing Silverback.

Growing old

Many people tell me that I look just like my dad,
For years this was the best compliment I ever had,
But having seen just recently, how this old man has changed,
Now when it is mentioned, I look at them deranged.

My hair is getting whiter, where dad is going bald,
He's going mutton jeff, he never hears you when he's called,
Even though the one part that's still growing are his ears,
He looks like baby Dumbo and compounds my darkest fears.

His back is bending forward, he now walks with a limp,
And the buggers shrinking, resembling a frail old gimp,
He's losing lots of weight now although won't hear my pleas,
Even though the arse of his trousers flop around his knees.

I know we all get older, but where has the time gone,
When was it that creaking bones and wrinkles crept upon,
Nowadays I look at dad and it's Granddad that I see,
And when I look into the mirror, dad stares back at me.

This is truly an irritation of the highest order that I had to write about. It happens all too regularly, and it pees me off every time.

Rush hour hold up

Pensioners line up on Wednesday morning
Just to annoy me
With tens of losing lotto tickets
Why can they not see
It's 8 o'clock in the morning
Rush hour to those who work
And they are holding up my queue
The silly cloth capped berks
Upon confirmation that
They've not won a single penny
Magically slips appear
To play this week there are so many
The lottery machine will bleep
A dozen times or more
But then they have to dig down deep
For money to pay for
At this point I am ready
To drop my Sun and leave
They will turn to apologise
Though this I don't believe
Lord above they have retired
They should still be in bed
Not holding up the rush hour queue
And messing with my head.

My in-laws took up bowls a few years ago, and we've gone to watch them on more than one sunny summers evening. It's worth going to see if only to have a bloody good laugh.

The Bowls Bunch

Whether it's flat or crown green bowls,
Old people in their whites,
Meet and get competitive,
Then put the world to right.

Standing there with jack in hand,
Ready to start the game,
Struggling to bend and send,
Because their back is lame.

Arthritis doesn't help,
When playing this gentile sport,
Especially on windy days,
When chills from draughts are caught.

How you send you bowl down,
Will be finger or thumb,
But how on earth can they tell,
When their extremities are numb.

"Measures" often gets called out,
And two more limp across,
To see which bowl is nearer,
With a roll of dental floss.

Two opponents mark the card,
Both trying to keep score,
Struggling to stay awake,
Cuz watching's such a bore.

Sometimes all the wrinklies,
Get so overheated,
Usually when the stocks of,
Tea and sarnies gets depleated.

When the match is over,
And the scores are validated,
They retire to lounge or bar,
And hope nothings dislocated.

Old folk and Technology

Old folk and technology should never be mixed,
Gadgets are too complex, they get their knickers in a twist,
Everything's remote controlled and adds to their confusion,
It's like trying to teach a chimp about nuclear fusion.

Try to show them how to use a mobile phones a hoot,
But this soon turns to anger and you want a gun to shoot,
You take the time to explain everything so crystal clear,
Then they'll try to make a call but photograph their ear.

Attempts are made to record TV programmes while they're out,
Instead of Loose Women they get Robson Greene fishing for trout,
Kitchen appliances being white confuses them much more,
Sometimes their washing falls out when you open the fridge door.

Video and DVD's, Blue Ray and MP3's,
Lawnmowers, hedge trimmers, and loppers for tall trees,
We know they have no clue, and no way to gauge,
Talk technology to the old folk's like speaking a foreign language.

Pensioners in the Supermarket

You'll see them there on any day
Wandering like lost souls
Ghosting up and down the aisles
Like poor demented trolls
A trolley pushed in front of them
A bag being pulled behind
Dressed ready for the Arctic
No I'm not being unkind
Ten of them will convene
In an aisle for a moan
You are in the Asda folk
Not the Darby and Joan
Others, without warning will
Stop dead in their tracks
Then look at you disapprovingly
If your trolley their legs smack
You find yourself apologising
Though it's not your fault
And as you walk away
You'll hear the faintest of insults
But it is totally different
When they barge into you
There'll be no apology
Kiss me arse or how are you
All this grief just because
They want to spend ten quid
On items that they need that day
It makes me blow my lid
Now you know the reason why
Shopping breaks my heart
I'd rather eat my own earwax
Than pre-empting these old farts.

The Little Old Girl

"Bloody Hell," the old girl cried,
As she slid down to the floor,
The barman said, "You've had enough,
You can't have anymore."

"How dare you speak to me like that,
You little sodding freak,
Pour some ale into me glass,
I've not had one all week."

The barman once again refused,
The old girl climbed the bar,
And tried to take his eye out,
With a smoldering cigar.

"Now then, that's enough of that,"
The pub manager said,
Then instantly regretted it,
As the ashtray hit his head.

The gaffers wife went for the phone,
The police force she would call,
The old girl lunged across the bar,
And forced the wife to fall.

She pinned the womans shoulders down,
Each shoulder with a knee,
The woman felt a sudden warmth,
As the old girl took a pee.

The gaffer saw all this transpire,
And finally saw red,
He wasn't particularly angry,
The blood oozed from his head.

The old girl reached up for a glass,
The gaffer's wife did flinch,
"Don't worry, I'll not hit you,"
Then a pint the old girl pinched.

Suddenly a booming voice,
Was heard across the room,
"Oh mother what you doing now,"
She felt impending doom.

Her son, a big lad, reached across,
And with one hand he lifted,
His mother like a little doll,
In fact she fairly drifted.

"How many more times mother,
Do we have to go through this,
I know you've had far more than one,
You stink of beer and piss."

"I only wanted one small drink,
The buggers all said no."
The son quickly apologised,
And turned around to go.

The gaffer shouted out "You're barred,
Look what you've done to us,"
The son apologised again,
His mother did just cuss.

"Now put me down, I've had enough,"
The old girl she did plea,
"Not til you behave yourself,
Christ's sakes you're ninety three."

Chapter 4

General Observations

This section covers everything else I can whinge or whine, praise or exult about. You may have realised by now that I have opinions about virtually everything. You can blame my Granddad for that (I've got to blame someone).

Here I cover topics such as Health, Holidays, Hobbies and Sport.

Observing my surroundings and trying to see the fun in what happens is something I do more and more as I get older. There is so much doom and gloom with everyday life, wherever I can find something to laugh at is a bonus. Laughing at myself is something I have learned to do more and more over the years. I've learned not to take myself too seriously, that way I give everyone else less to take the pee out of.

I really hope you enjoy this selection.

A Hospital Visit

I traveled to the hospital,
My ill friend there to visit,
I hadn't been there very long,
In fact only a minute.

No sooner than I had arrived,
His lips they had turned blue,
He lay there gasping for his breath,
I knew not what to do.

I grasped his flailing waving hands,
And patted reassuringly,
His eyes were glazing over now,
He lay and stared right through me.

I placed my head against his chest,
To listen for his heart,
There was the faintest of noise there,
To panic I did start.

I checked his wrist and then his neck,
For a pulse, this was surreal,
So sure I was that he would die,
For nothing could I feel.

Panic rose in me once more,
And I screamed out for a nurse,
I screeched so loud it scared me,
That my friends eardrums would burst.

Then suddenly his hand shot up,
And grabbed me round the head,
Then using superhuman force,
He pulled me toward the bed.

As he pulled me closer,
The death rattle I heard,
I reached up for his buzzer,
And the rest is quite absurd.

He looked at me with eyes so red,
Then his hand did swipe,
He shouted "Get your bloody feet,
Off my oxygen pipe!".

Post Op Pain

Whilst lying in my hospital bed,
My body still being racked with pain,
I had the most awful lest feeling,
That I'd have to go through this again.

For something inside me was nagging,
That something was rather amiss,
That somehow, something had gone badly,
Or that someone had taken the piss.

Then shortly the nice surgeon fella,
Came sidling up to the bed,
And I mentioned the pain I was feeling,
From the tips of my toes to my head.

His answer took some time in coming,
And the look on his face was quite sad,
For he knew that he'd dropped quite a clanger,
And the news he'd to give me was bad.

I said to him "Now come come doctor",
"Can you not give it to me straight",
He mumbled that he'd get right to it,
But then he proceeded to wait.

The longer I waited I knew it,
That I hadn't much time left on this coil,
And soon I'd be packed processed worm food,
Buried in a box 'neath the soil.

I asked him if it was a cancer,
Or a tumour causing this distress,
But the medic shook his head quite vehemently,
And confirmed it was more of a mess.

The sweat was a pouring out from me,
It seemed to come from every pore,
I was in early stages of panic,
Whilst not really knowing the score.

"I came in for a tonsillectomy,
You said that it would all be sound",
He responded "You had a vasectomy",
Cos some daft prat turned the bed round.

Private Examination

Walking in the surgery, the doctor smiles at me,
I tell him that my problem is it burns me when I wee,
He asks me to drop my kegs and fetch my old man out,
As I do my willy hangs and limply flops about.

My GP then gets a pen and notes he starts to write,
Giving me assuring glances that I'll be alright,
Out comes the prescription pad to give me medication,
His attention to detail enforces his dedication.

I am then asked questions, about how long since when,
And I explain in detail that it happens now and again,
The GP then refers to a large book stood on his desk,
Then tuts a little as though he's being bothered by a pest.

Then he fetches a glass wand from out of his top drawer,
And uses it to lift my dick then lowers as before,
He then tells me he cannot be sure of what he sees,
I said "Well it's a certain fact it's not a bloody budgie."

Endoscopy

To the hospital I did go,
And have a test so it would show,
What was causing discomfort,
When food traversed towards my stomach.

On the bed I did lie,
As I was asked on my left side,
The throat spray that was used to numb,
My epiglottis now succumbed.

Like a huge liquorice lace,
The camera was put in place,
The doctor said it wouldn't hurt,
Then air into me he did squirt.

It brought a tear to my eye,
As I reached 120 psi,
My belly now no longer flopped,
It got so big I thought I'd pop.

A piñata personified,
Although no presents held inside,
I expected Spanish kids with sticks,
To line up just to knock me sick.

More air into me was pumped
And then at once I belched and trumped,
I tried to apologise,
As methane stung the nurses eyes.

Once the procedure was finished,
And my belly had diminished,
Never more do I want to see,
A doctor for an endoscopy.

I originally wrote the following for a work colleague before she started maternity leave. My intention was to offer help and advice, because that's the kind of guy I am, but I'm not sure it had the desired effect.

Having a Baby!

You are having a baby, and boy can't we all tell,
You're at elephantine proportions, but you are still looking well,
Now giving birth's a frightful thing, it's full of pain and sweat,
So I'm going through the stages for you, so you won't forget.

At first you'll feel some twinges, around your nether bits,
Then shooting pains will pulsate through you, in starts and fits,
Then comes the time your waters break, the child makes its first mark,
There's so much fluid you expect to see, old Noah in his Ark.

You must get to the hospital, the journey's not too far,
But first you have to fathom out, how to squeeze into the car,
Decorum out the window now, your hormones hit sky high,
You throw yourself on the back seat, and how you land you lie.

Arriving at the hospital, you start to plan ahead,
How to get out of the car and then clamber on the bed,
"Here comes the big white whale", you expect to hear them say,
You're strapped onto a gurney and then promptly whisked away.

The delivery suite is bright and there are huge lights all around,
But what you're really aching for, is very quickly found,
The magic mask that fit's the mouth and helps dull all the pain,
Momentarily you're floating, so you breathe in hard again.

Contractions they keep coming, they're coming thick and fast,
The baby's on the move now, you think you're there at last,
But life is never straightforward, and the pains start to subside,
And now you start to fret a bit, and your poor hubby you'll chide.

Then as before the pain comes back, a little stronger now,
You're pushing with all your might, to get it out somehow,
Then he lovingly takes your hand, and tries to get you panting,
You look at him with fiery eyes, and once again start ranting.

You feel more and more uncomfortable, so he tries to assist,
By plumping up your pillows, but you try to break his wrist,
Cos that's the way he'll share your pain, if possible at all,
Or if through his back passage, he could pass a bowling ball.

Then after 12 more hours, of this sheer heavenly bliss,
Your baby makes its final move, to escape its abyss,
You push again with all your might, you face turns shades of blue,
You are scared that if you break wind, that you may just follow through.

Then he moves down to the business end, and shouts "Here's the head",
You want to yank the bugger out, and get off the sodden bed,
With one last push, you here a gush, a cry, the baby's here,
Welcome now to motherhood, it's now you shed your tears.

Then he says "Bloody hell, the boy's hung like a bear"
The midwife laughs "It's your daughters umbilical cord lying there"
She then hands him the scissors, to detach the tot from you,
The last 12 hours have been rough, but you saw it through.

The baby is laid on your tum, you see for the first time,
This wonderful little being, covered in all kinds of slime,
Then the midwife, with a tug, the placenta she removes,
And checks all nine segments are there, and shows it you to prove.

The really freaky thing about new born babies is wild,
All babies look like Gandhi and Churchill just had a child,
They look up at you and recognise the one thing they love best,
Then open up their tiny mouths to latch onto the breast.

Now you are a mother, and a fine one you will make,
A couple of months from now, and you'll be baking bread and cake,
I wish you all best wishes, with everything you do,
I'm sure it won't be long before you're planning number two.

This poem is all about our first holiday abroad, as a family. We travelled to Lido di Pomposa, near Rimini, by coach, which going was wonderful as our transport was half empty. The journey back was awful because the coach was full to bursting.

Jacques le Boule, Italy and a Sophia Loren wannabe

When I was 16 years old,
My little sis and I were told,
That we were going to Italy,
For this years annual holiday.

The apartment was okay,
But so basic in every way,
We were on the first floor you see,
And we did have a balcony.

The Brits who were with us were grand,
And we made such a happy band,
We spent each day down at the beach,
Our cares and woes well out of reach.

The women were left to sunbathe,
While us men sloped off to play,
Boules in a huge sand pit,
At least 'til we got bored with it.

One day Jacque le Boule, or Jack,
Looked liked he was having an attack,
We followed the direction of his stare,
To see a Godess showering there.

For a good ten minutes or more,
Our boules sitting there on the floor,
A bunch of dirty old men,
Watching this 'Sophia Loren'.

The girl resembled this great legend,
While this bunch of new found friends,
Could not help but watch this beauty,
A real curvaceous Italian cutie.

When this Sophia Loren wannabe,
Stopped, we dashed off to the sea,
This is an endearing memory,
Of our time in Italy.

The Bulls go to France

Mr and Mrs Bull and their tribe of sixteen kids,
Decided on a holiday abroad,
Mr Bull spoke with a friend of a friend,
For a vehicle big enough for his horde.

They hired a lovely chalet in Northern Brittany,
And promptly set off for the port,
Their journey averaged over 100 mile per hour,
Eight police forces did report.

Once they parked their vehicle on the ferry,
To the bar the Bulls descended,
And drank for the duration of the crossing,
Many tables were upended.

They drove the first 10 miles or more,
On the left side of the road,
The Gendarmes quickly corrected the Bulls,
But let go of this crowd.

The chalet was clean when the family arrived,
Within minutes the placed was trashed,
Mr Bull drove off to the local town,
To get his giro cashed.

At the post office, he belched "Au revoir",
To the pretty girl behind the screen,
She paid out the money and reeled from his breathe,
Pungent because his teeth were green.

Mr Bull staggered to the bar next door,
And downed two bottles of house red,
Then got behind the wheel of his van,
And set off cuz he needed his bed.

When he got back to the now knackered chalet,
His tribe were annoying the neighbours,
He shouted at them to keep the noise down,
As he lurched and fell through the front door.

The very next day the Bulls were arrested,
An incident had been reported,
The British Government had to get involved,
And the Bulls were duly deported.

The Red Sock Gang

This is the legend of the Red Sock Gang,
Both feared and revered throughout the land,
They quaff ale all day 'til they fall on the floor,
They drink a pub dry then they move on for more.

Raymundo is chief of this well watered click,
But hates when referred to as an alcoholic,
He won't lose his temper or use words profane,
But silently gas you with a cloud of methane.

Second in command is Tony 'One Can',
Who reconnoiters better than any man,
With his eyes peeled and a finely tuned ear,
He guarantees where is sold the cheapest of beer.

Kenny G it is my duty to report,
Can cut a man down with a witty retort,
With a brain as huge as his shovel like hands,
His tongue is too sharp for any normal man.

I am the youngest member of this bunch,
And I'll sing for my supper, or breakfast, or lunch,
As the ale flows the song just drone on,
Your ears feel like they've been assaulted upon.

So the next time you are out in your town,
And espy four strangers please take a look down,
And if the socks worn are the brightest of red,
Do a quick 180, go home back to bed.

Holiday Searching

I think I'll go on holiday,
But don't know where to go,
I've got me here some brochures,
So soon I think I'll know.

I look at France, but I don't like,
The arrogant buggers ways,
They're so condescending,
And they eat frogs legs all day.

And I can't bare going to Belgium,
It's only just north of France,
And Holland is too bleeding flat,
So that aye got a chance.

I'll have to bypass Germany,
World Wars put paid to this,
They eat saurkraut and bratwurst,
And the beer's as week as piss.

Now Austria and Switzerland,
Are both covered with snow,
And Scandinavia is too cold,
Tis where the North winds blow.

Now Spain I think is far too hot,
It wouldn't be much fun,
I'd burn all of me tender bits,
And smear on aftersun.
And Portugal is right next door,
That too is off the list,
I look at the Balearics,
Those too I'll give a miss.

Italy does not interest,
Nor anywhere round the Med,
But I've got to go to foreign shores,
Or I will lose my street cred.

Malta loves us British,
but the island aye that big,
And Greece is just too far away,
So I couldn't give a fig.

So now I'll look at Ireland,
But they're far too laid back,
And I aye too keen on Guinness,
Cos it turns me poo jet black.

And then I look at Scotland,
An idea with which I'll flirt,
But I cannot understand them,
And the men up there wear skirts.

Next I'll cross off Wales,
My views on this I'll air,
This is a place where men are men,
And all the sheep run scared.

So I'm left with good old Blighty,
Where it rains and we all moan,
Oh bugger it, I'll save me dosh,
And spend two weeks at home.

The Phantom Crapper

Staring down into the pan,
This wasn't passed by a normal man,
So I set out to see if I can,
Seek out the Phantom Crapper.

As I look down in the bog,
I think it must be one hard slog,
Trying to pass this Redwood log,
For the Phantom Crapper.

Looking around the office space,
For telltale signs in a colleagues face,
Cuz what is dropped is a damn disgrace,
By the Phantom Crapper.

Whoever's dropping these large turds,
I know this may sound so absurd,
But some the size of massive birds,
Dropped by the Phantom Crapper.

To this day I have not found,
He who can without a sound,
Pass through his hole a good ten pound,
Who I call the Phantom Crapper.

Please tell me now is it you,
Are you the very person who,
Keeps banging out these monster poos,
Are you the Phantom Crapper?

Mistaken Identity

"Come on in," said the nubile girl,
As she stood there at the door,
A see through nightie she did wear,
So I looked down at the floor.

I entered very cautiously,
And tried hard not to stare,
When her night attire rode right up,
To reveal her rear so bare.

"Come on, sit down and have a rest,"
"I have something for you,"
And then she slipped her nightie off,
To reveal a lot more too.

"I think you have got this all wrong,"
I tried in vain to plea,
But she thrust her bosom in my face,
And sat upon my knee.

Gyrating there upon my lap,
Her hand upon my zip,
Momentarily the blood did rush,
As she kissed me on the lips.

She pulled herself away from me,
And lay there on the floor,
The slightest groan from her escaped,
As she gyrated some more.

Her limbs were flailing everywhere,
Her torso twisted, turned,
Her body manically convulsed,
The carpet her skin burned.

And then as if by magic,
A can of spray cream appeared,
She squirted here, she squirted there,
The cream on her was smeared.

Then various bits of fruit came next,
Covered from head to feet,
She lay there like a huge dessert,
Good enough to eat.

But at this point I must admit,
My ardour it did plateau,
For I didn't really fancy,
Romping with a human gateaux.

I then remembered why it was,
I came here to this place,
I got up very quickly,
And to the door did pace.

She called for me to stay awhile,
She hadn't finished yet,
For there were more ingredients,
She'd found them on the Net.

"This is how you wanted me,"
"You said this was your fetish,"
"Now get back here, while I finish,"
"And stop being a big wet lettuce,"

I told her that she was mistaken,
That we'd never met before,
She flew into a rage and screamed,
I'd emailed six times or more.

I explained politely that this was,
Mistaken identity,
This was my last call for the day,
Then I was off home for my tea.

That all this started just before,
I'd had a chance to greet her,
I was sent here by the Gas board,
Simply to read her meter.

Road Rage

Late one foggy autumn night driving my Mini Cooper,
Visibility was barely zero yes this was a true pea-souper,
Following the hazy fog lights of the car in front,
Ensuring not to get too close in case I caused a shunt,
On I went through cotton wool, my head craned left and right,
What a time for fog to descend this late of a night,
Trying so hard not to speed as conditions got much worse,
Brake lights in front lighting up make my language terse,
Like a Meerkat so alert with my eyes opened wide,
This chap is driving like a twat I quietly deride,
Speeding up then slowing down he's being rather rash,
I wouldn't be surprised if he ends up suffering with whiplash,
Then suddenly right out the blue he comes to a direct stop,
I stand up on my anchors as I start to blow my top,
I rush out of my Mini and threaten to skin him alive,
He said "I'm sorry mate, but I've just parked up on my drive!"

I would just like to point out that the following is NOT a true reflection of my sister! Mandy's much worse!!!

Younger Sister

I have a younger sister, who gets right on my wick,
Because she bites her nails, and her nose she always picks,
She is certainly no lady, I'd say she has no savvy,
And when she walks, everyone thinks she is an Irish navvy.

She farts and grunts and belches and makes other noises obscene,
It doesn't matter where you are, you can tell where she has been,
She's loud and does just what she wants, she's often out all night,
And all the guy's are wary of her, in case she wants a fight.

You'll never see her in a dress, or anything ladylike,
She's used to being in leathers, when she's on her motorbike,
It would be nice to smell the hint of perfume at the least,
But what you get with little sis is the stench of axle grease.

She goes to our teams home games to hurl abuse at the ref,
And every second or third word has to begin with the letter F,
She's smoking like a chimney, she's on sixty fags a day,
Her teeth are as brown as Daddies sauce, her breath reeks of ashtrays.

I've seen more graceful elephants, I have smelt sweeter bogs,
And in the looks department I've seen more beautiful warthogs,
And if you ever meet her be sure not to stare,
At the tufts of hair and blemishes that appear here and there.

John Merrick would have turned her down if she'd asked for a date,
The stench of her is so putrid, even the blind do hate,
Her BO's overpowering, one's eyesight becomes blurred,
She smells so bad she could knock a fly off a freshly dropped dog's turd.

But after all is said and done, she is still my little sis,
And I truly love her to bits although I take the piss,
Cos she'll lovingly look at me with her one good eye,
And I see through all her defects, there's a heart of gold inside.

Who's in charge?

Gazing at the television that's fixed to the wall,
Images and noises from within the box do pour,
Vivid colour fills your sight, you hear every note,
And watch the adverts umpteen times so you never misquote.

An infinite selection of crap real life TV,
Is churned out by TV companies for you and me,
Prime time programme scheduling is taken up by soaps,
And cheaply made offerings that offer little hope.

Cookery, celebrity, docu-soaps and dance,
Kaleidoscope to keep you in a deep hypnotic trance,
The more you watch, the more you stay there glued fast to your seat,
It doesn't matter that you're viewing old sixties repeats.

Frozen in a cryogenic state, remote in hand,
A multimedia package that also includes broadband,
There's over 700 channels from which to choose your viewing,
Hours can be spent surfing but still the trash keeps spewing.

Every now and then you'll uncover a natural TV gem,
From an age when variety was the crème de la crème,
But in the main TV programmes are not good by and large,
And you have to ask is it you or your TV that's in charge?

Am I Going Round The Twist?

Am I going round the twist,
Feeling scared I clench my fist,
To fight an enemy I can't see,
The one that's sitting within me.
Is it lying in my brain,
Where sometimes I am in great pain,
Confusion reigns when it plays tunes,
And shadows creep across my moon.
Lethargy keeps setting in,
I try to move but still can't win,
But I refuse to be defeated,
Even if I can't be treated.
Life insurance will not touch,
Although I doubt I'm worth that much,
This now impacts on family,
The ones who will look after me.
It could just all be in my head,
The pathway that I fear to tread,
And that there's actually nothing wrong,
And should have known it all along.
So while my sanity's intact,
I'll state it now as a matter of fact,
That if another lesion appears,
I'll fight it my remaining years.
I know I'm surrounded by love,
Both here on earth and heaven above,
And while this love coarses through me,
I will not yield on bended knee.
Putting this on paper though,
Has helped to pass half hour or so,
Half hour more the tunes don't drone,
Half hour less before I'm home.

A Pigeons Life

"Pigeons find a mate for life",
A little gem I've learned,
And recent goings on I've seen,
Have made me quite concerned.

For there are two such pigeons,
Perched upon my garden fence,
The goings on I'm about to tell,
I hope won't bring offence.

There are several times each day,
They sit at the same spot,
And indulge in their conjugals,
They do not care one jot.

First of all they make a noise,
Whilst eyeing up the other,
Then they peck each others face,
A birdy snog 'n smother.

Then she seems to brace herself,
For the upcoming strife,
And lowers her body to the fence,
To hold on for dear life.

Then up he jumps on to her back,
His talons keep him steady,
He wriggles around alittle until,
The signal that he's ready.

And then his wings are opened wide,
"Look at me!" he says,
Trying to keep his balance,
While his mate, and my fence sways.

Then he finishes the act,
And promptly hops right off,
They both sit there alittle while,
She lights a fag, he coughs.

He walks awkwardly along the fence,
She sorts her feathers out,
He puffs out his little chest,
It's enough to make you shout.

And then, just when you think,
They're going to fly back to their den,
He struts right over to her side,
And starts it all again.

The Bucket

Waking up at 3am and bursting for a pee,
I couldn't put the light on or my dad would shout at me,
Fumbling around in the dark for the metal rim so cold,
The bucket we used as the upstairs loo cuz our house was so old,
Feeling for the freezing rim, beginning to kneel down,
If my thumb hit water, I'd immediately frown,
Aiming for the centre a splashing sound soon starts,
Occasionally my privates touch the rim which make me smart,
With a little breaking wind my wee starts to decrease,
A yawn and then a shudder follow, completing my relief,
And as I shuffle back to bed, I take the time to ponder,
How on earth do mom and sister manage that? I wonder.

Will You Be My Friend

Will you be my friend?
I've not gone round the bend,
I have so much to offer you,
If you will be my friend,
I'll care for you, look out for you,
I'll take you to the pub,
And if you're really up for it,
We'll eat expensive grub.
Will you be my friend?
I'll try not to offend,
If you will give me just one chance,
By becoming my friend,
I'll buy expensively lavish gifts,
I'll treat you like a royal,
You've never met no one like me,
You'll see I'm really loyal.
Will you be my friend,
On me you can depend,
I'll be your rock when things look black,
Oh please become my friend,
I've waited such a long, long time,
Will you come for a walk?
Just agree to meet with me,
And I'll promise not to stalk.
You will be my friend,
It'll happen in the end,
Cos you will have no say in it,
Oh you will be my friend,
Just like all the others,
On which I've set my sights before,
So come on now, there's no escape,
Just open your front door.

That Daft Cat

Here I am its half past ten and I'm whistling in the yard,
Trying to get the cat in, who'd have thought it'd be so hard,
In my hand a box of munchies I frantically shake,
Enticing her with the bait, hoping she will take,
It's bloody cold out here but I'm determined I will win,
The battle of wits I've started, no I will not give in,
That daft cat of mine will have to learn that I am in charge here,
Why'd I buy a black cat I just cannot see her,
I'm pretty sure she's fairly close for I can hear the bell,
I attached to her collar which I thought made her look swell,
Now I've reached for the tin of Kit-e-Kat that's there,
And a fork to tap it, now that noise fills the air,
I am sure the neighbours think that I'm losing the plot,
But you see I live alone, the cat's all that I've got,
She knows it too the little sod, on her I do depend,
I wished that I'd taken more time and picked a better friend,
Suddenly I see the green of her eyes in the dark,
Dancing down the garden path, fireflies having a lark,
I hear her meow, the little call that says she's on her way,
She'll fill her belly and settle down at the end of her big day,
After she has eaten, she curls up on my lap,
She purrs contently while I stroke her as she takes a nap,
I think about this game we play as the day comes to an end,
I wouldn't be without her, this daft cat I call my friend.

A former work colleague asked me to write something fun for her old school friend, who was having a rough time at home in their native South Africa. They both appreciated it, I think!

Cheer Up!

Whenever you are feeling down,
And true friends just cannot be found,
In fact there's no one else around,
Just think of me in England.

Harsh words it seems are being spoken,
You feel your life is just a token,
And then you find your TV's broken,
But I am here in England.

You get a cold and you start sneezing,
Your breathing quickly turns to wheezing,
But over here I'm bloody freezing,
In my home in England.

You may not know where to go,
Your mood swings always to and fro,
But you are not wading through snow,
Like I am here in England.

And whenever you're feeling pain,
Ank think your are going insane,
At least you are not drenched by rain,
As I am here in England.

To make you feel a lot less sad,
Was the idea I originally had,
But now I'm feeling twice as bad,
Cuz I'm here in England.

Because you are a real true friend,
Your broken heart I'll help to mend,
Before I go "round the bend",
Living here in England.

So cheer up, and try being bright,
This verse should help I hoped it might,
But be warned you will get a fright,
When you visit me in England.

Merry Christmas!

Tis that special time of year, when Santa makes his calls,
Racing through the midnight sky while he stares at Blitzens balls,
Trying to ensure that all the presents he departs,
And hoping that he can survive the cold and Reindeers' farts.

There he stands all dressed in red and ready for the off,
He checks one last time that none of his Reindeer has a cough,
Cuz there is nothing known to man that's worse than Reindeer flu,
Especially as when they cough too hard they follow through.

With all the presents in his sack, it's late on Christmas Eve,
The clock strikes on the hour and it is now time to leave,
He snaps the reigns and Rudolph sighs, the journey they commence,
And Santa has to pull hard right to miss his garden fence.

Then with a hearty "Ho Ho Ho", they speed into the night,
Trying to avoid the planes, for fear of giving fright,
Swooping down to land when a delivery he makes,
Ensuring that he does not pull too hard when he brakes.

Santa made that mistake once, and never will again,
It's not clear what hurt more, humiliation or the pain,
One minute he is happy and grinning from ear to ear,
The next he is extracting himself from Vixens rear.

The night goes by so slowly so that he can do the rounds,
The Reindeer are feeling the strain, he's put on a few pounds,
His belly's getting bigger and his trousers are too tight,
Rudolph's nose is shining cuz he blocks out the moonlight.

And so the night draws to a close, he's very nearly done,
Trying to stay awake to dodge the poo is half the fun,
But knowing that on Christmas morn, all children will be chuffed,
He heads home quite contentedly, as well as feeling stuffed.

Upon landing at his home, his wife turns on the light,
Because her hubby is home after working through the night,
And when he spies her, his grin does return from ear to ear,
We've all heard about the fact that Santa comes but once a year.

I Don't Like Drinking Anymore

I don't like drinking anymore,
Because it makes my head feel sore,
My stomachs like a tombola,
You don't get that from drinking cola.

Alcohol makes you do daft things,
The weak feel strong, the tone deaf sing,
Introverts get up to dance,
Extroverts strip down to their pants.

Little men Goliath become,
And want to take on everyone,
Some become loving and sweet,
Others collapse and go to sleep.

I myself have been all these,
And at the time it seemed a wheeze,
Next morning a penance you'll pay,
And lose most of the next two days.

I thought my friends would understand,
The choice I made now I'm a man,
I hoped that they would follow me,
And live their lives alcohol free.

Now at the pub when we arrive,
I'm the grumpy one because I drive,
I start at 6 and finish at 4,
I don't like drinking anymore.

I Wish

I wish I was a pigeon,
Soaring so high in the sky,
I would look down upon the world,
And poop right in your eye.

I wish I was a kitten,
I'd curl up on your lap,
I'd wretch and cough a fur ball up,
Then have a little nap.

I wish I was a puppy,
I'd learn to sit and beg,
Whenever you have visitors,
I'll go and shag their legs.

I wish I was your baby,
I'd coo because I'm happy,
And then I'd bang a big one out,
And squash it in my nappy.

I wrote this for my work colleagues a couple of years ago. It went down well so I thought I'd include it.

A Merry Christmas Eve!

To all my friends and colleagues,
I take the time to write,
A poem to help remember,
What will happen Christmas Eve Night.

Children will be in bed by six,
For fear of hearing bells,
The following hours you will spend,
Trudging the stairwells.

Placing presents under trees,
Some placed there for you,
You shake and squeeze your gifts,
And hope they offer you a clue.

The Christmas lights still twinkle,
A little brighter than before,
But this is cos the tree has shed,
Pine needles on the floor.

You sit and arrange presents,
Into groups so all can see,
That the smallest pile of gifts there
Are the ones addressed to thee.

The doorbell is heard ringing,
And you jump up from the floor,
"We wish you a Merry Christmas",
Starts as you open the door.

That's all you get for 50p,
Oh my how things have altered,
As kids we would sing all Carols,
Until our little voices faltered.

But tell me this, if you can,
What is Christmas all about?
Is it about religion?
Or drinking til you pass out?

Or is it about eating,
Everything you can,
To put on weight alarmingly,
To become twice the man.

Is it just for Children?
Seeing their little faces glow,
This must be the true meaning,
For my bank balance tells me so.

Is this the time for peace on earth,
And for goodwill to all,
So why is it that I still cringe,
When neighbours come to call.

Or is it about adorning,
Homes with lights in many ways,
The National Grid works overtime,
As some turn night to day.

Like me you too may ponder,
About all this and more,
Wandering if more singers,
Will come carolling at your door.

Then tiredness overtakes you,
It's very nearly twelve,
You view the scene around you,
and you feel like Santa's elf.

Though your scences are fading,
You will still espy,
Santa's gifts the child has left,
The milk and the mince pie.

Once the pie is eaten,
Crumbs left on the plate,
The milk helps wash the pastry down,
To bed you go, it's late.

You dream of a time when you believed,
In the bearded man in red,
Who visits good kids once a year,
In a Reindeer driven sled.

You are woken early,
By a dazzling beaming smile,
And all the pains of Christmas fade,
And it all now seems worthwhile.

"He's been!" you hear the screeching,
As the sleep's rubbed from your eyes,
And in that special moment,
You come to realise.

You see that's the truest meaning,
Of Christmas I can see,
We all help bring the magic,
To all kids like you and me.

I hope you all enjoy,
Your little bit of Christmas heaven,
And I wish you Merry Christmas,
And propserous 2007.

Pugilism

When I reached my late teens a pugilist I became,
I was billed "The Real Deal" which I'd use as my ring name,
My first few months spent training so my manager could see,
How I'd cope with the rules of the Marquis of Queensberry,
Then the time came for me to take on my first fight,
And it was booked in my home town for a Wednesday night,
I arrived at the venue, a pubs function room upstairs,
Before me stood the ring and island in a sea of chairs,
The poster confirmed that my bout was the third of six,
Against a guy from Nottingham, against whom I'd pit my wits,
The dressing room a cellar, my seat a PA speaker,
There were no windows, no fresh air, could tonight get any bleaker,
The time came for my bout and I headed out towards the ring,
Friends and family in the crowd did chant and cheer and sing,
Then came my opponent, he had muscles in his spit,
And when he grinned his teeth had hair which frightened me a bit,
The first of six rounds started with me trying to keep away,
From my gargantuan muscle bound adversary,
The end of round bell sounded, the crowd weren't a happy bunch,
The first three minutes over neither boxer threw a punch,
Round two started I got brave and hit him on the chin,
He stood there while I winced at the pain I was now in,

He lunged at me and caught me with a right hand uppercut,
Three teeth quickly left my mouth and landed on his foot,
I got up the count was 6 and spat blood in the air,
The referee then punched me cos it landed in his hair,
At the beginning of the third he pummelled into me,
I threw a punch at fresh air as I fell down to my knees,
I got up at the count of 5 but still was seeing stars,
He then connected with a punch that dropped me on my arse,
Luckily the bell then rang, that was the end of three,
"Thank God we've reached the halfway point" my trainer said to me,
At the beginning of the fourth he caught me on the chin,
He hit me so hard I had to pay to get back in,
By the time I reached the ring the count reached 66,
Just my luck to get a ref who likes to take the piss,
Sitting on the speaker when back in the changing room,
My trainer did his very best to try to lift the gloom,
"I know you will be hurting lots for the next day or five",
I was glad I managed to get out of there alive,
So that one fight spelled the end of my boxing career,
I needed four teeth fitting and they sewed back on my ear,
My nose had to be re-set and I now walk with a limp,
Bent double knuckles dragging I now look just like a chimp.

Cup Final 1992

Between the ages of 21 and 26, I played competitive football in the Walsall and District Football League for a great team called Tamebridge. We enjoyed a successful spell, the zenith being winning the league and cup double in the 1991/92 season. I want to dedicate this to all the lads who were there that wonderful day. The team line up was as follows,

1   John Kelly
2   Andrew Read
3   Andrew Mason
4   Darren Jones
5   Ian Stewart
6   Derek Auburn
7   David Jones
8   Steve Alford
9   Gary Auburn
10 Chris Phillips (c)
11 Steve Bailey

Subs were Wayne Gleeson and Jason Cooksey.

My dad was sponge man for the day and took great pride in his involvement with the team, something that Tamebridge would acknowledge at the end of the season, when the awarded him a special trophy as a thank you for all he'd done for the team.

The following is an account of the cup final, where we beat the Railway 2-0.

Cup Final 1992

It was 19th of April in the year 1992,
When Tamebridge turned up at Oak Park with nothing left to prove,
Already the League Champions, now looking for the double,
To add the Divisional Cup title shouldn't really cause much trouble.

Tamebridge lined up in their Celtic like strip of green and white,
The Railway like Kilmarnock, kitted out in blue and white stripes,
Neither team looked nervous in the cool spring morning air,
They had met twice this season and were currently all square.

Two minutes gone, Tamebridge got a free kick down the right,
Ian Stewart stepped up to the ball and right footed gave it flight,
The ball half cleared reach Stevie Bailey out in the left wing,
Who crossed the ball into the box, for someone to head it in.

Steve Alford met the ball and flicked it across the box,
The ball ran across me as I lined up for a shot,
I managed to keep the ball in play and pass it to Dave Jones,
Who fell very awkwardly, we all heard his moans.

Wayne Gleeson came on as sub as Dad helped Dave away,
The game restarted with a goal kick coming down our way,
A few more minutes passed by and we won a free kick,
Just inside their half and Taffy went to do the trick.

The ball was lofted in the box, a defender headed out,
It fell to Chris Phillips our cap, who gave it such a clout,
The sprout bag bulged, it nearly broke, the ball was hit so hard,
It went so fast their keeper stood there like a lump of lard.

Their next attack came via a throw in down our left hand side,
Then our keeper shouted something that chilled my insides,
Johnny Kelly shouted out "Andy Read's got two",
Their left winger turned to me and asked me "Is it true?"

Several minutes later Chris attacked down our left wing,
Turned their right back inside out with the talent he did bring,
Then he tried to cross the ball, which hit the poor guys arm,
We shouted for a penalty, the referee not alarmed.

Chris just took no notice and crossed the ball again,
Into the six yard area where we had two men,
The ball reached Gary Auburn, our fantastic goal machine,
And he duly buried it, the goal doubled our lead.

The Railway fought back really hard, but we defended well,
The half time whistle sounded, it was our day we could tell,
The match shortly restarted and the game flowed end to end,
At times all our players called upon to frantically defend.

We had many chances and we could have scored five more,
As both teams took turns to break down the oppositions walls,
Then with just two minutes left Ian Stewart cut his head,
Jason Cooksey replaced him as the pitch ran blood red.

The final whistle finally blew and Tamebridge won the cup,
We retuned to the Tiger pub for a celebratory sup,
This was the year we won the double with this team so fine,
Tamebridge in the history books as one of the best of all time.

Get Fit Regime

I'll go jogging every morning,
To get my system going,
And after only half an hour,
Like an old man I'll be blowing.

I'll try so very hard to keep,
Myself from being unfit,
But end up sweating like a pig,
And feeling really shit.

I need to do this now you see,
Because I'm getting older,
I'll work towards a six pack,
Instead of this hard boulder.

I really want to keep in trim,
I want to get in shape,
I want this slob before me,
To let Adonis escape.

My body will be a temple,
I hope to get there soon,
It's currently a restaurant,
Or worse a greasy spoon.

I'll cut out all the chocolate,
The fry ups and the chips,
I want to see my feet again,
And get back my slinky hips.

I'll try to build up muscles,
Where currently resides fat,
Because I am all wobbly,
And I'm feeling such a prat.

I'll spend more time at the gym,
I will work so much harder,
My partners kicked me into touch,
Because I've lost my ardour.

I'm getting fit to win her back,
I'll do it if it kills,
And just to help me on my way,
I've started popping pills.

I've got to get this body toned,
My physique to revamp,
I want to build my torso,
So when I sneeze I get cramp.

I want to see my reflection,
And experience the highs,
I want to be able to crack walnuts,
Right between my thighs.

I want to be so muscle bound,
And lift three times my weight,
Where currently I puff and blow,
Lifting an empty milk crate.

I know that I'll soon get there,
That I will reach my dream,
I'll start properly tomorrow though,
When I've finished the crispy creams.

I am a lifelong Walsall fan, it is my home town club after all. This is my tribute to Walsall FC, which is also my take on the famous style of poem which starts "Tomorrow I went to the pictures . . ."

Walsall FC

Next week I went to watch Walsall,
To play an away game at home,
We were winning 1-1 at half time,
I saw a voice behind me moan,
"I am fed up with shellin aht money",
"To come eer and see em fer free",
"They just am not value for money",
I argued that I did agree,
The half empty ground was a sell out,
The pitch was a bone dry mud bath,
The ref handed cards out like Christmas,
To the crowd who had incurred his wrath,
I made my way in to the pie shop,
I was thirsty and fancied a drink,
They gave me a pie with no pastry on,
And I got indigestion I think,
I re-took my seat on the terrace,
As the second half got underway,
I saw no more goals in the second half,
Cuz I was facing the right way,
We ended up taking all 3 points,
For a very outstanding nil-nil,
I may watch my team again last week,
Because they are so bad they're brill.

In the summer of 1999, I started a small sided soccer team, Reads United, appropriately named. Here's what we were about.

Reads United

This is the story, about how a team,
Became football league champions, and fulfilled our dream,
It took us five seasons, in fair and foul weather,
It almost took us, to the end of our tether,
A fine group of men, lined up proud and true,
And out on the pitch, we knew what to do,
And match after match, we racked up the wins,
And we wouldn't give up, nor we wouldn't give in,
Our squad was world famous, at least in Walsall,
Renowned for our tactics, upon which we'd mull,
Right from the kick off, we'd win every ball,
Looking for team mates, listening for calls,
Fight for possession, raking that pass,
Trying so hard, not to fall on your ass,
Winning the headers, tackling hard,
Looking for spaces, stealing a yard,
The goals kept on coming, we conceded so few,
The points kept increasing, with each game anew,
Then the last week arrived, and we were confused,
We had back to back games, we were not amused,
We needed one win, from the games we had left,
But we drew the first, we were feeling bereft.

The next team arrived, to take their best shot,
Whilst they were ready, we certainly were not,
And our legs grew heavy, as the game wore on,
With the scores still level, our chances had gone,
Then suddenly a hopeful, punt up the park,
Found our defender, who was having a lark,
Could he score the goal, that gave us the lead,
Or would he collapse, or get a nosebleed,
The next bit seemed to run in slow mo,
He drew his leg back, then let it go,
The ball seem to float, up towards the net,
But we new for sure, the shot couldn't be met,
The ball passed the keeper, I can now divulge,
How I nearly cried, when I saw the net bulge,
The final whistle blew, and we'd won the league,
We were jumping for joy, and forgot our fatigue,
We collected our trophies the following week,
Then went off for a new venture to seek,
And to date all these years down the line,
We still haven't equalled that season so fine,
But that season I'm sure will never leave me,
When Reads United created our own history.

Nan loved her wrestling, but got a little hot under the collar when the bad
guys appeared, which was every damn bout.

Armchair Wrestling

Every Saturday afternoon,
At around 4pm,
World of Sport showed wrestling,
Nan fired up again.

"Welcome to you grapple fans",
Kent Waltons smooth tones purred,
Never knowing the full extent,
Of the wrath that was incurred.

Whenever Mick McManus fought,
Nan would shout and curse,
Then put me in a headlock,
Like I'd tried to pinch her purse.

How I've not got cauliflower ears,
Is a mystery to me,
Nan put me in a Half Nelson,
If sat upon her knee.

Giant Haystacks would appear,
And fire and brimstone shot,
She'd cuss and blind even more,
And totally lose the plot.

Big Daddy entered the ring,
Nan would cheer and clap,
A minute into the first round,
I'd be in a Boston Crab.

I was scared if the bad guy won,
Cuz Nan her fists would clench,
At this time I'd sidle away,
And hide under a bench.

When the wrestling finished,
My Nan returned to me,
The red mist that had clouded her,
Now nowhere to be seen.

My Heroes

I've always enjoyed football,
And playing the guitar,
So my biggest heroes,
Are two of the best by far.

Gary Moore plays the blues,
He is the best I've seen,
His fingers nothing but a blur,
No one quicker there has been.

Bobby Moore was captain,
Of our champs of '66,
Getting past this maestro,
Needed more than Pele's tricks.

I've tried to emulate these men,
When enjoying both my hobbies,
But I play football just like Gary,
And guitar more like Bobby.

Waiting in the Surgery

Waiting in the surgery to see my GP
A sweet little old lady parked her bum next to me
Coughing, sniffing, grumbling, and sneezing
Two generations of asthmatics wheezing.

With a sneeze sputum shot out her gob
There on the wall a green virus riddled glob
Then a tattered tissue from her pocket did appear
She wiped the mess from the wall while mumbling "Oh dear".

Chapter 5

Sidney

Sidney is a character I have created, loosely based on someone very dear to me. All of Sidney's adventures and experiences actually happened, although I have elaborated a little for comedic effect.

Sidney was a quiet man, was never any trouble to anyone, and was so laid back he was almost horizontal. In fact he could be sat next to you and you probably wouldn't know he was there.

The most animated I ever saw him, was whenever my dad visited. Sidney would be out of his chair sparring, bobbing a weaving. It was like watching Alan Minter and Charlie Magri getting ready to fight!

Admittedly this chapter will mean more to my close relatives than anyone else, but still I think you'll warm to Sidney.

Sidney and the Air Raid Shelter

Enjoying the evening summer son,
Watching butterflies fluttering fun,
Peacefully puffing away on his pipe,
Sidney sat pondering his wonderful life.

Resting his back while sat on the floor,
On an old air raid shelter from the second world war,
Her reached for the tea cup down at his left side,
And noticed that there was nothing inside.

Trying to figure when he last had a sup,
Releasing a groan he pulled himself up,
Sitting in sunshine was such a toil,
So he popped to the loo while the kettle did boil.

While he was sat there he heard such a din,
Two womens voices were screaming for him,
He pulled up his kegs and raced back outside,
And could not believe the scene he espied.

Where he'd been sat so quiet and no trouble,
The shelter had toppled and turned into rubble,
His wife abd the neighbour with tear in their eyes,
Turned around slowly and to their surprise.

Because there stood Sidney, all four feet ten,
And smile returned to their faces again,
"We thought the shelter had crushed you, you see"
Sid was so grateful, for needing more tea.

Sidney and the Smoking Shed

Sidney had always smoked a pipe,
"I'll pack up smoking" he told his wife,
His penknife and pipe were locked in a draw,
The baccy was binned it was needed no more.

A hobby was needed to help to distract,
So a large shed was put in the garden out back,
With a radio and a calor gas fire,
Sidney enjoyed his "me time" acquired.

One autumn evening in the twilight,
Dolly looked out and got a real fright,
The shed out back was enveloped in smoke,
Sidney was trapped in a fire the poor bloke.

With steely resolve she broke down the door,
Expecting to see Sidney laid on the floor,
But what she saw gave her the shock of her life,
Sidney peacefully puffing away on his pipe.

A Roaring Fire on a Summers Day

Back when coal fires were the fashion,
A well stoked one was Sidneys passion,
One built with meticulous care,
Which would superheat the surrounding air.

Passing birds would often try,
To miss the flames shooting up to the sky,
In Summer, Winter, Autumn and Spring,
Sidneys fire always welcoming.

I remember one hot summers day,
You could get tanned from the strong suns rays,
We visited Sidney who was at rest,
His right foot placed on the chimney breast.

Not only did the fire so roar,
He'd opened the windows and the front door,
We said of pure madness this is shear,
And Sidney replied "I know but it's so hot in here!"

Sidney's noisy habit

Sidney enjoyed his time alone,
When the only one at home,
For his hobby was to sit,
And play his classical music.

From Gustav Holst to Beethoven,
He would listen over and over,
Sidney had no earphones,
For miles you'd hear the drone.

His record carefully selected then,
Turned the volume to 11,
The houses foundations would shake,
I'm sure that once the dead did wake.

One time I went to visit him
The door opened, I walked right in,
He said while puffing away on his pipe
"Oh how I do love a peaceful life"

Sidney the Minder

Sidney in his later years,
Lived in Milton Place with Dolly,
And every evening they were joined,
By Renee who was jolly.

She'd sit with them an hour or two,
The women chewing the fat,
Sidney drifted off elsewhere,
He preferred his life like that.

He'd be called back to this Earth,
When Renee was about to leave,
And he'd get his shoes and coat on,
While a few sighs he would breathe.

Renee lived two doors away,
And Sidney walked her home,
Dolly thought she'd be attacked,
If she went alone.

Now at just about four feet ten,
You'd go a long way to find a,
Chap as small as Sidney,
Who was prepared to be a minder.

Sidney goes courting

Sidney was a little man, he stood just four feet ten,
And his love for Dolly he proved time and time again,
When he courted Dolly, who stood at five feet six,
To reach her for a goodnight kiss he had to stand on bricks.

Every evening he would make an effort for his girl,
His trousers ironed ready to take his Dolly for a twirl,
He would always look his best, he never took a chance,
He would even iron the turn-ups in his underpants.

Dressed in his best whistle and flute, Sidney looked just swell,
Looking forward to seeing Doll who always scrubbed up well,
They'd trip the light fantastic, both Sidney and his girl,
Because of the size difference it was Sidney who was twirled.

Sidney had to catch the bus, because he could not drive,
He spent half his wages keeping his love alive,
Finally he asked Dolly if she would be his wife,
In his inimitable way, peacefully puffing on a pipe.

Chapter 6

Limericks

I have always enjoyed listening to and reading Limericks so I thought I'd have a go a composing a few myself.

Limericks are a way of rhyming anything with everything without the need to make too much sense of it all.

See what you think of these:

There was a young man from Penzance,
Who gave his ex a second chance,
But she bored him rigid,
Cuz she was too frigid,
And wore Bridget Jones underpants.

A midget who lived in Iran,
Was so small that he lived in a can
But one day he slipped,
The lid sliced his pips,
And now he's only half a man.

A beautiful French girl named Claire,
Had a penchance for chocolate éclairs,
Carried under her arms,
When days were so warm,
Cream would matt her armpit hair.

There once was a girl named Andrea,
Who suffered terrible diarrhoea,
She set off for the trap,
Cuz she needed a crap,
But deposited there, there and here.

There once was a handsome young Greek,
Whose awful BO made him reek,
"It's not me", he said,
With a shake of his head,
"cuz I use deodorant once a week!"

There was an old lady called Rene,
Whose house was impeccably clean,
She wielded her duster,
With all she could muster,
Then have to cool down with ice cream.

There was once an old dear called Dot,
Who made coffee in a teapot,
It was made with cold water,
And her son and her daughter,
Were convinced she was losing the plot.

There was a young girl from Peru,
who for weeks hadn't managed a poo,
so her doctor did give,
her strong laxatives,
and the next day she lost 1 stone 2.

There was an old man from Brazil,
Who spent his whole life eating trill,
In the coldest of weather,
He sprouted with feathers,
And proceeded to chirp, squawk and shrill.

There was this young fella called Mark,
Who exposed himself in the park,
One night while he flashed,
His old man was gashed,
By a nail he'd not seen in the dark.

One job that I fancied when young,
As a Butcher I felt I'd belong,
Because I did fancy,
Having girls ask me,
If I could give them some tongue.

There once was a woman from Gloucester,
Who bought a kitten them lost her,
Next day it turned up,
Looking just like a pup,
And she didn't notice the impostor.

There was an old gentleman Bill,
Who asked for the Viagra pill,
At the Darby and Joan,
All the old dears there moaned,
When Bill with his pill tried to thrill.

There once was a young man named Lee,
Whose lover was seventy three,
But he did protest,
That when kissing her breast,
He would get a mouthful of knee.

There once was an old man named Bob,
Who had an unusual job,
Because he joined the crew,
Of the new QE2,
As the foghorn he'd got a big gob.

A young window cleaner named Martin,
Could not climb ladders without farting,
He once followed through,
Caked the windows in poo,
The pain that he felt left him smarting.

There was a worried mum named Pam,
About the size of her little girl Sam,
Cuz the legs of her daughter,
Retained far more water,
Than is held at the Kielder Dam.